SUPERWOMEN in STEM

Women scientists in Medicine

NANCY DICKMANN

raintree

a Capstone company — publishers for children

Raintree is an imprint of Capstone Global Library Limited, a company incorporated in England and Wales having its registered office at 264 Banbury Road, Oxford, OX2 7DY – Registered company number: 6695582

www.raintree.co.uk
myorders@raintree.co.uk

© Brown Bear Books Ltd 2021
This edition published by Raintree in 2021

Created by Brown Bear Books Ltd
Text and Editor: Nancy Dickmann
Designer and Illustrator: Supriya Sahai
Editorial Director: Lindsey Lowe
Children's Publisher: Anne O'Daly
Design Manager: Keith Davis
Picture Manager: Sophie Mortimer
Printed and bound in India

ISBN 978 1 4747 9862 4 (hardback)
ISBN 978 1 4747 9868 6 (paperback)

British Library Cataloguing in Publication Data
A full catalogue record for this book is available from the British Library

Concept development: Square and Circus / Brown Bear Books Ltd

Picture Credits
Alamy: Chronicle 20; Getty Images: Vittoriano Rastelli 35; istockphoto: 16, 28, 40, Steve Debenport 5; National Portrait Gallery: 10; Public Domain: 4, Douglas Glass 29, Ludwig Grillich 26, Maryland State Archive 14, Mount Holyoke College Archives and Special Collections, South Hadley MA 38, New York Library Archives 17, Carl Pietzner 27, US National Library of Medicine, Department of Health, US Government 41, US National Park Services 39; Shutterstock: Ariana Mera 33; Thinkstock: istockphoto 32, 34; Wellcome Images: 8, 9, 11, 15, 21, 22, 23.

Character artwork © Supriya Sahai
All other artwork © Brown Bear Books Ltd

Every effort has been made to contact copyright holders of material reproduced in this book. Any omissions will be rectified in subsequent printings if notice is given to the publisher.

All the internet addresses (URLs) given in this book were valid at the time of going to press. However, due to the dynamic nature of the internet, some addresses may have changed, or sites may have changed or ceased to exist since publication. While the author and publisher regret any inconvenience this may cause readers, no responsibility for any such changes can be accepted by either the author or the publisher.

contents

medicine through time

The human body is complex, and people have always tried to understand how it works. Scientific discoveries have shown us how to heal and protect ourselves.

Early people knew very little about how the body worked. They used herbs and other natural materials as medicines, and they also relied on spiritual healers. However, there is evidence that people were drilling teeth and performing some surgeries more than 6,000 years ago.

Long before they were allowed to train as doctors, women worked as nurses and healers.

Women doctors are now just as qualified as men thanks to the determination of many brave pioneering women in the past.

EARLY MEDICINE

By about 2,000 years ago, medicine was becoming a science. Doctors in Egypt, Rome, Greece and China were developing new ideas about health. Some of their ideas were wrong, but other treatments were successful. A few doctors cut open dead bodies to find out how they worked. As the centuries passed, doctors made important discoveries. In 1628, William Harvey figured out the system that pumps blood around the body. By the 1900s, discoveries such as antibiotics and anaesthesia were helping to save many lives.

MAKING THEIR MARK

In many cultures, women have a long history of using herbs and other natural remedies, passing down their knowledge from one generation to the next. But in the 1400s and 1500s, only people who had trained at universities were allowed to practise as doctors in many countries. At that time a university education was not open to women. Women were limited to nursing the sick and delivering babies. However, by the late 1800s female doctors began to take their rightful place alongside men.

florence Nightingale

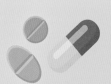

In the 1800s, nursing was not seen as a suitable career for wealthy women. Florence Nightingale changed all that, and helped thousands of people.

Florence's parents were wealthy, so they could afford to travel. They were in Florence, Italy, when their second daughter was born, and they named her after the city. When they returned to England in 1821, Florence and her sister Parthenope grew up in a happy home. Florence's father taught her about history and literature, but Florence had to fight to be allowed to study maths, which was seen as an unsuitable subject for girls. However, Florence got her own way in the end.

❝ Were there none who were discontented with what they have, the world would never reach anything better. ❞

NURSING

Girls like Florence were expected to marry and raise a family, but she wanted to help people. As a teenager, she decided the best way to do this was by becoming a nurse. Her family didn't agree, but Florence was determined. In 1850 she travelled to Germany for training. On her return, she got a job overseeing a women's hospital in London. She proved to be just as good at running a hospital as she was at caring for patients.

THE CRIMEAN WAR

In 1853, war broke out between Russia and the United Kingdom, who had France and Turkey on their side. The fighting took place on the Crimean Peninsula. Reports soon came back that wounded soldiers were not getting the care they needed. The British public demanded that something be done, and in 1854 Florence travelled to the Crimea with a group of 38 nurses.

Some wounded or sick soldiers were taken away from the fighting in the Crimea by boat. They were sent to hospitals to receive treatment.

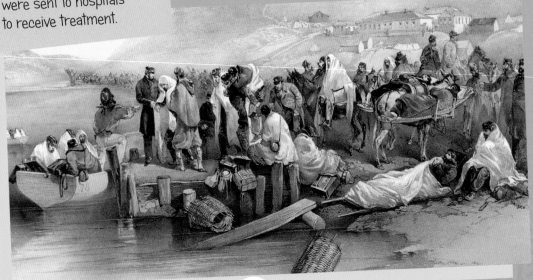

Florence became famous with the soldiers for being "the Lady with the Lamp".

SQUALOR IN SCUTARI

Florence arrived at the military hospital in Scutari, Turkey. There she found a dirty hospital full of rats and fleas, with not enough soap, bandages or healthy food. She soon realized that more patients were dying from disease and infection than from their wounds. Florence and her nurses cleaned the hospital, organized a laundry service and arranged for a cleaner water supply.

Thanks to their dedicated care, death rates at the hospital began to drop. Florence worked tirelessly, checking on her patients through the night by the light of her lamp. She also kept detailed records of everything her staff did and kept the hospital running smoothly.

Shortly after Florence arrived, the hospital was overwhelmed with wounded soldiers from two major battles. She called the hospital the "Kingdom of Hell".

MARY SEACOLE

In 1855, another woman arrived in the Crimea to help the sick and wounded. Mary Seacole (1805–1881) was the daughter of a Scottish soldier and a Jamaican woman. Mary grew up in Jamaica, where her mother taught her about traditional healing that used herbs as medicine. When Mary grew up, she and her husband ran a boarding house in Jamaica. She worked hard, and during her spare time she nursed patients.

Jamaica was part of the British Empire, and when the Crimean War began, Mary decided to travel to the UK and volunteer as a nurse. But no one would hire her, so she bought her own medical supplies and set out for the Crimea.

Mary wrote a book about her life and nursing career, which became a bestseller.

When Mary arrived, she met Florence Nightingale, who offered help and advice. Mary built an establishment that she called the "British Hotel". It sold healthy food, clothing and blankets to the soldiers. Mary also provided nursing assistance when needed. She was very popular with the troops, who raised money for her when she went back to the United Kingdom after the war.

STATISTICS

Florence had always been good at maths, and she began to put these skills to good use. She used the careful records she kept in Scutari to analyze the best ways to improve general medical care. To get support for her ideas, she needed to convince the public, and she knew that columns of numbers wouldn't work. Instead, she used the figures to draw statistical graphs and charts that were easy for anyone to understand.

RECOGNITION

Florence's work in the Crimea made her a celebrity. After the war, she returned to the UK, where she kept working to improve hygiene and health. In 1860, she opened the Nightingale School of Nursing in London, which still trains nurses today.

Florence lived to the age of 90. Every year, International Nurses Day is celebrated on 12 May, her birthday.

Elizabeth Blackwell

Elizabeth Blackwell started her career as a schoolteacher, but she became the first woman ever to graduate from medical school.

Elizabeth was born into a large and happy family in Bristol on 3 February 1821. Her father had a sugar refinery and the family was able to afford private tutors for the children. Elizabeth loved reading and learning. When she was 11, a fire destroyed her father's refinery. The family set sail on a seven-week ocean voyage to the United States and started a new life there. The family first settled in New York, but after a few years they moved to Cincinnati, Ohio.

QUICK FACTS

NAME: Elizabeth Blackwell

BIRTH: 1821, Bristol, UK

OCCUPATION: Physician

EDUCATION: Geneva Medical College

13

> 66 It is not easy to be a pioneer – but oh, it is fascinating! I would not trade one moment, even the worst moment, for all the riches in the world. 99

SUPPORTING THE FAMILY

The sugar-refining industry relied on sugar cane harvested by slaves in the West Indies. Elizabeth's father was against slavery so the family moved to Ohio, where slavery had been abolished, to grow sugar beets without the help of slaves. But soon after arriving in Ohio, Elizabeth's father died, leaving the Blackwells almost penniless.

TEACHING SKILLS

To help support the family, Elizabeth and two of her sisters set up a school for young women. They were able to earn enough money to keep the family together. The Blackwell sisters closed their school in 1842, but Elizabeth continued to teach students privately. Soon afterwards, she took a job as a teacher in Kentucky.

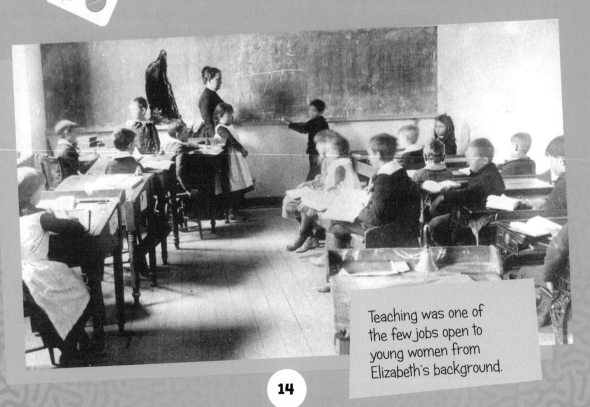

Teaching was one of the few jobs open to young women from Elizabeth's background.

Elizabeth was the first woman in the United States to earn a medical degree.

A NEW DIRECTION

While Elizabeth was teaching in Kentucky, a conversation with a dying friend changed her life. Her friend told her that she wished she could have been treated by a female doctor – but at that time, there were no women doctors. Elizabeth decided that becoming a doctor would be a good way to help people. She took more teaching jobs to earn the money for medical school.

At first Elizabeth found that no medical school wanted to accept a woman as a student. She received one rejection letter after another from the leading medical schools. Finally, in October 1847, she was accepted at Geneva Medical College in New York. Some of the townspeople and students treated her badly, but she did not give up. When Elizabeth graduated in 1849, she was top of her class.

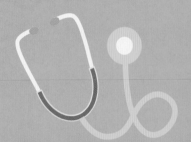

66 **None of us can know what we are capable of until we are tested.** 99

SHATTERED DREAMS

After her graduation, Elizabeth decided that she wanted to train as a surgeon. She knew that to do this she would first need more on-the-job experience. She travelled to Europe and found work at a maternity hospital in Paris. Unfortunately, one day she was treating a baby with an eye infection when she got pus in her left eye. The eye became infected and Elizabeth went blind in that eye. Her dreams of being a surgeon were over. Elizabeth went to London to work in another hospital and think about her future.

At St. Bartholomew's Hospital in London. Elizabeth studied under the famous surgeon James Paget.

New York City's many poor people were in desperate need of affordable medical care.

BACK IN THE US

Elizabeth returned to the United States in 1851 to settle in New York. No one was willing to hire her as a doctor because she was a woman, so she started her own medical practice and also gave public lectures. She wanted to spread her belief that good hygiene could keep people healthy. In 1853 she opened a clinic for women in one of New York's slums. Four years later, Elizabeth and her sister and another female doctor turned the clinic into a successful hospital.

LATER CAREER

In 1868, Elizabeth achieved a lifelong dream when she set up a women's medical college in New York. The next year she moved back to the UK, where she started a successful medical practice. In 1875 she became a professor at the London School of Medicine for Women. Throughout her career, Elizabeth wrote and gave lectures, doing her part to improve standards of health. She died in 1910.

During her time in London, Elizabeth met the nurse Florence Nightingale, who would soon become famous for her work with soldiers in the Crimean War. The women became good friends.

Elizabeth Garrett Anderson

Another Elizabeth also wanted to be a doctor. She was a pioneer for women in the United Kingdom, and inspired a generation.

Elizabeth Garrett was born on 9 June 1836, in Whitechapel, London. Her father was a successful businessman who believed in education for all his children, not just the boys. Elizabeth was taught at home while she was young, then went to boarding school as a teenager. But the school didn't teach much science or maths, which Elizabeth wanted to study. The students there were expected to marry and become mothers, not doctors, so they were taught mainly English, French and "good manners".

❝ When I felt rather overcome with my father's opposition, I said as firmly as I could, that I must have this or something else, that I could not live without some real work. ❞

FINDING HER WAY

After finishing school, Elizabeth continued to study on her own. She had a close circle of female friends, who often discussed women's rights. At that time, women in the UK could not vote, and very few jobs were open to them. Elizabeth and her friends wanted women to have the right to study at universities, and to vote. In 1859, Elizabeth met Elizabeth Blackwell and was inspired to study medicine. But no women in the UK had yet received a medical degree.

TRYING TO GET IN

Elizabeth worked for several months as a surgery nurse at Middlesex Hospital, and was allowed to observe operations. But when she tried to enrol in the hospital's medical school, she was turned down.

One of Elizabeth's friends was Emily Davies (pictured here), who founded Girton College, Cambridge, in 1869. It was the first college for women in the UK.

Throughout her life, Elizabeth was determined to overcome any obstacles in her path.

In 1860 Elizabeth studied medicine with private tutors while sending off applications to other medical schools. They all turned her down. Although Elizabeth's mother was horrified at the idea of her daughter becoming a doctor, her father finally supported her.

THE SOCIETY OF APOTHECARIES

Elizabeth eventually figured out a solution. The Society of Apothecaries couldn't award a medical degree, but by passing their exam she would get a licence to practise medicine. More importantly, their rules did not forbid women from taking the exam. In 1865, Elizabeth passed her exam with a high score, becoming the first woman in the UK to be certified to practise medicine. The Society quickly changed its rules so that other women were unable to follow in her footsteps!

In 1876, a new law was passed in the United Kingdom. It allowed British medical authorities to grant a licence to all qualified applicants, regardless of their gender.

In 1865, there was an outbreak of a disease called cholera in London. People were so desperate for medical care that they were even willing to see a female doctor.

MAKING HER OWN WAY

Elizabeth now had a medical licence, but still no one would hire her. Hospitals didn't want female doctors. Elizabeth set up her own medical practice, and in 1866 she opened the St. Mary's Dispensary for Women and Children. This hospital had an all-female staff and was for poor female patients. A few years later Elizabeth took time off to finally get her MD (Doctor of Medicine) degree from the University of Paris. She was the first woman ever to receive one.

FIGHTING FOR WOMEN'S RIGHTS

Throughout her life, Elizabeth supported women's rights. In 1871, she married James Skelton Anderson, and they had three children. At that time, married mothers only worked if there was no other way of supporting the family. Women like Elizabeth, whose husband had a good job, were not expected to work. But James was supportive of Elizabeth's career, and she continued to work as a doctor while raising their children. She was an example for other women.

This building in London was the site of the first St. Mary's Dispensary for Women and Children.

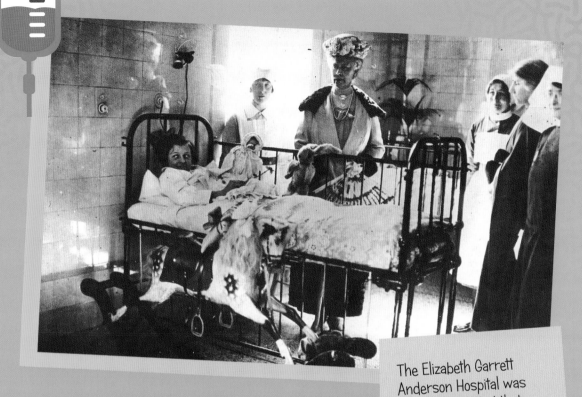

The Elizabeth Garrett Anderson Hospital was so well respected that even Queen Mary visited patients there.

TRAINING MORE DOCTORS

The dispensary that Elizabeth set up became the New Hospital for Women, serving many patients. In 1874, she joined with Elizabeth Blackwell and other doctors to found the London School of Medicine for Women. It was the first medical school in the United Kingdom to train women as doctors, and one of the students was Elizabeth's daughter Louisa, who graduated in 1897. But Elizabeth wasn't finished with firsts. She and her husband eventually retired to the town of Aldeburgh, and she became the mayor in 1908, the first female mayor in the UK. After Elizabeth died in 1917, the hospital that she set up was renamed in her honour.

melanie klein

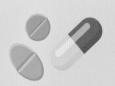

Melanie Klein studied psychoanalysis and developed groundbreaking new theories by studying the behaviour of children.

Melanie Reizes was born into a middle-class Jewish family on 30 March 1882. She was the youngest of four children. Melanie was very close to her older sister Sidonie, who died when Melanie was only four. Melanie had a stormy relationship with her mother, who had a strong personality. These early difficulties may have contributed to the depression that Melanie suffered all her life. Her father was a dental surgeon, and Melanie wanted to go to medical school too. However, she gave up that dream when she got married at the age of 21.

QUICK FACTS

NAME: Melanie Reizes Klein

BIRTH: 1882, Vienna, Austria-Hungary

OCCUPATION: Psychoanalyst

EDUCATION: Self-taught

66 In even very young children [there is] a capacity for insight which is often far greater than that of adults. **99**

MARRIED LIFE

Melanie's husband, Arthur Klein, was an engineer, and they often moved because of his work. They had three children: Melitta, Hans and Erich. Unfortunately, the marriage was not a happy one. Melanie regretted giving up the chance to qualify as a doctor, and her father and her brother had died in 1900 and 1902, causing Melanie further unhappiness. She threw herself into her studies in an attempt to fill the emptiness in her life.

A NEW DIRECTION

The family moved to Budapest in 1910, and Melanie discovered the writings of Sigmund Freud. He had developed psychoanalysis, a way of treating mental problems by analysing unconscious mental processes. A few years later, Melanie started receiving treatment from the Hungarian psychoanalyst Sandor Ferenczi. He encouraged her to think about how psychoanalysis could be applied to children.

The ideas of Sigmund Freud were seen as controversial, but they were also hugely influential.

In 1919, Melanie presented her first paper to the Hungarian Psychoanalytic Society. Two years later she moved to Berlin, where she treated patients and continued her research. She and her husband got divorced soon after. In 1926, Melanie moved to London, England, where she had many supporters for her ideas about psychoanalysis.

Melanie found married life and motherhood difficult. and she tried many different treatments for her depression.

OTHER PIONEERS

Melanie was not the only woman to study the psychoanalysis of children. Karen Horney was a German psychoanalyst who followed Freud's theories at first. She eventually began to disagree with some of his ideas, especially those to do with women. She explored the ways in which anxiety as a child could lead to problems later in life. Freud's own daughter, Anna, also became a psychoanalyst after starting her career as a school teacher. She took what she had learned about children from observing her school students, and applied it to her own methods of psychoanalysis.

66 **We must always remember to learn from yesterday, live for today and hope for tomorrow.** 99

PLAY THERAPY

One of the problems with psychoanalysing young children is that they can't answer questions about their feelings and actions in the same way as an adult can. As a way of solving this problem, Melanie developed the technique of play therapy. She believed that young children express themselves through play more than through words. By watching children play and draw, she could learn about their unconscious anxieties and feelings.

Many of today's child psychologists still use play therapy with young children as a way of learning about and helping their patients.

LATER CAREER

As Melanie continued to develop her ideas, she worked with both children and adults. Since events and relationships in childhood affect a person's mental state as they grow to be adults, treating adults helped Melanie develop her theories about children.

Although her career was successful, Melanie still faced difficulties. Her son Hans died in a climbing accident. Her daughter, Melitta, also became a psychoanalyst, but she disagreed with many of her mother's theories. A rivalry sprang up, and they were never reconciled. Melanie died in 1960, at the age of 78.

Melanie's pioneering work continues to influence the psychological treatment of children today.

OBJECT RELATIONS THEORY

Melanie is probably best known for her work on developing what is called "object relations theory". In this theory, "object" means a person or event in the unconscious mind that shapes how a person relates to situations and other people later in their life. Melanie's theories emphasized the importance of a child's relationship with his or her mother, and examined how the relationship changes over time.

Rita Levi-Montalcini

Rita Levi-Montalcini didn't want to treat patients –
she wanted to learn about how our bodies work.
Her discoveries paved the way for new treatments.

Rita was one of twin girls born on 22 April 1909, in the northern Italian city of Turin. She and her sister Paola had an older brother and an older sister. Their parents loved learning and culture, and they encouraged their children to read and learn about the world. However, their father was very old-fashioned. He believed in different responsibilities for men and women. Although he wanted his daughters to learn, he didn't want them to go to university or have careers.

NAME: Rita Levi-Montalcini

BIRTH: 1909, Turin, Italy

OCCUPATION: Neurobiologist

EDUCATION: University of Turin

31

> 66 **Above all, don't fear difficult moments. The best comes from them.** 99

GETTING HER WAY

By the age of 20, Rita knew that she wasn't cut out to be a wife and a mother. She wanted independence and a career, and she wanted to study medicine. Rita worked hard, studying Latin, Greek and maths. An even harder job was convincing her father to let her go to university, but she succeeded. Rita earned her MD from the medical school of the University of Turin in 1936. Her work had focused on the nervous system, and she took a job as a research assistant for one of her professors.

FACING PERSECUTION

Times were changing in Italy. Benito Mussolini, the Italian leader, had turned the country into a fascist dictatorship, with himself in complete control.

The city of Turin, which was once Italy's capital, lies at the foot of the Alps.

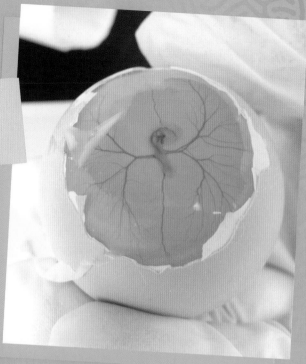

Rita researched the ways that nerves developed in chick embryos.

In 1938, Mussolini introduced new laws that stated that people of Jewish heritage could no longer work at universities or in professions such as medicine. Rita's family was Jewish, so she lost her job. She set up a laboratory in her bedroom and continued her research. When World War II began in 1939, the fighting forced her family to move from Turin to the countryside, and later to Florence.

AFTER THE WAR

American and British troops took control of Florence in 1944, and Rita was hired as a doctor. She worked in a refugee camp that was home to people who were fleeing the fighting in the north. When the war finally ended in 1945 she returned to Turin and her research. In 1947 Viktor Hamburger, a professor at Washington University in St. Louis, invited Rita to move to the United States to work with him.

While working in her bedroom laboratory, Rita made some of her own tools. They included surgical instruments made from sharpened sewing needles.

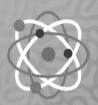

33

66 After centuries of dormancy [inactivity], young women... can now look toward a future moulded by their own hands. 99

FINDING ANSWERS

At Washington University, Rita spent long hours in the lab. One day she noticed that a tumour from a mouse, which she had transferred to a chicken embryo, had caused nerves to grow rapidly. Rita's theory was that the tumour was releasing a substance that was stimulating nerve growth. With another scientist, Stanley Cohen, she was finally able to isolate the substance, which they called nerve growth factor (NGF).

RECOGNITION

Rita and Cohen discovered NGF in the 1950s, but it took other scientists years to realize that their discovery could lead to new medical treatments. It wasn't until 1986 that Rita and Cohen were awarded the Nobel Prize in Physiology or Medicine.

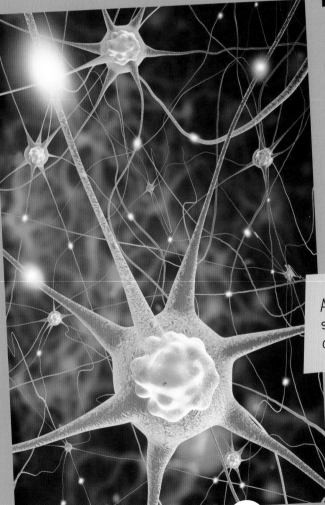

A network of nerve cells sends messages between different parts of the body.

Throughout this time, Rita had kept busy. In 1962 she founded the Institute of Cell Biology in Rome, and divided her time between Italy and St. Louis.

In 1992, Rita and her twin sister Paola founded a charity to provide education for girls in Africa. Ten years later, she founded the European Brain Research Institute. Rita lived to the age of 103, and never stopped her research work. She was always looking for more answers about how the human body works.

In recognition of her achievements, Rita was made a lifetime member of the Italian Senate.

NERVE FACTOR

Nerve growth factor (NGF) is a protein-like substance that nerve cells use to communicate with each other. It helps nerve cells to grow and survive in the body. The discovery of NGF helped scientists figure out more about how the nervous system works. By studying how NGF interacts with other substances, scientists today hope to develop new treatments for brain tumours, Alzheimer's disease and other conditions.

Virginia Apgar

Virginia Apgar was a leader in the fields of anaesthesiology and birth defects. She also developed a test still used on most babies born today.

Virginia was the youngest of three children and was born in New Jersey, United States, on 7 June 1909. Her whole family loved music, and she learned to play the violin, a hobby she enjoyed for the rest of her life. Like the rest of her family, Virginia was active and full of energy. She was known for her endless activity, and for talking as fast as her mind raced! Her father was an amateur inventor, and Virginia showed an interest in science too. By the time she was in secondary school, Virginia knew that she wanted to be a doctor.

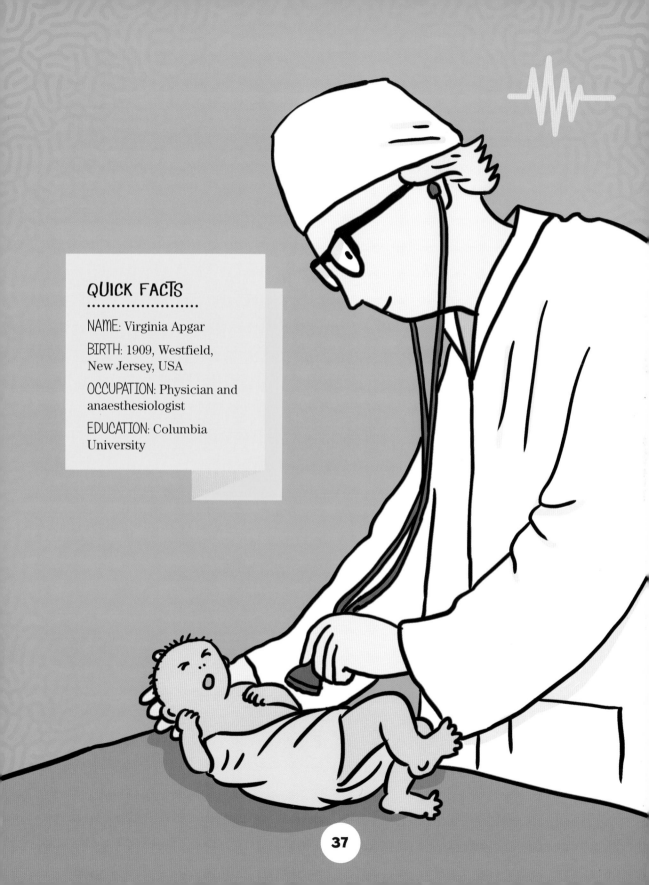

QUICK FACTS

NAME: Virginia Apgar

BIRTH: 1909, Westfield,
New Jersey, USA

OCCUPATION: Physician and
anaesthesiologist

EDUCATION: Columbia
University

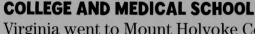

66 Nobody, but nobody, is going to stop breathing on me. **99**

COLLEGE AND MEDICAL SCHOOL

Virginia went to Mount Holyoke College, where she studied zoology. She also had part-time jobs, played in sports teams and joined an orchestra – and still got top grades! After graduating, she went to medical school at New York's Columbia University. She was one of just nine women in a class of 90. She started training as a surgeon, but one of her lecturers thought there would be few jobs for female surgeons. He encouraged her to focus on anaesthesiology instead.

ANAESTHESIOLOGY

Nurses were usually in charge of anaesthesia during an operation. However, anaesthetic drugs and techniques were improving all the time, and using them required more training than nurses were normally given. Virginia was among the first doctors to train in anaesthesia.

The educator Mary Lyon had founded Mount Holyoke in 1837 as a school for women. She wanted to educate all women, not just the rich.

As anaesthesia improved, it allowed surgeons to perform longer, more complicated operations.

After she finished her studies, Virginia returned to Columbia to help set up the first anaesthesia department at its hospital. It was a big job: she had to recruit and train medical students, organize research projects and oversee the use of anaesthesia during surgery.

APGAR THE TEACHER

Virginia turned out to be a popular and talented teacher. She helped compile a textbook on anaesthesiology, and she taught her students as they accompanied her on her rounds each day. In 1949, she was appointed a professor, giving her more time to spend on teaching and research. She began to focus on the use of anaesthesia on women in labour. Virginia researched its effects on their babies. She hoped to find ways to lower the death rate among newborns.

Virginia's close friend L. Stanley James said this about her: "She was loyal and generous, always dependable, and ready to help those in crisis."

66 **Do what's right, and do it now.** 99

INFANT DEATH

In the 1950s, the overall death rate for babies was going down, but many babies were still dying in their first 24 hours of life. Virginia's research showed that lack of oxygen was one of the major causes. She believed that if doctors could be trained to assess and monitor the newborn's health, survival rates would be higher. She developed a scoring system that would help them assess the baby quickly.

THE APGAR SCORE

The system became known as the "Apgar score". There were five categories on which a newborn would be scored as 0, 1 or 2. The maximum score is 10, for a healthy baby. Most hospitals score a baby at one minute and five minutes after birth.

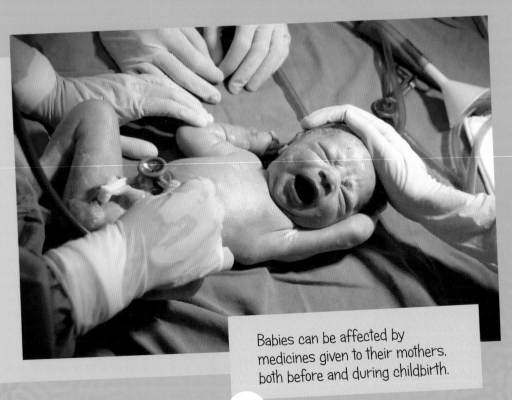

Babies can be affected by medicines given to their mothers, both before and during childbirth.

APGAR SCORE

	0	1	2
heart rate	no heart rate	fewer than 100 beats per minute	more than 100 beats per minute
breathing	not breathing	weak cry and slow breathing	strong cry and breathing
reaction to airways being suctioned	no response	grimace	grimace and pull away
muscle tone	floppy	some flexing of arms and legs	active motion
colour	blue or pale all over	bluish hands or feet	good colour all over

BIRTH DEFECTS

In 1959, Virginia was offered a job with a non-profit organization known as the "March of Dimes". She was put in charge of research into how to prevent birth defects and how to take care of children who were affected by them. Virginia's energy, experience and people skills made her the perfect person for the job.

Virginia continued to teach, and also to learn, taking courses on genetics in her sixties. She died in 1974 at the age of 65, leaving behind a rich legacy. The score named after her is still used in hospitals around the world.

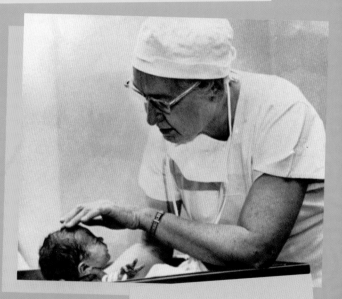

Virginia examines a newborn baby in the late 1950s.

Timeline

1805	Mary Seacole is born in Kingston, Jamaica.
1816	René Laennec invents the stethoscope.
1820	Florence Nightingale is born in Florence, Italy.
1821	Elizabeth Blackwell is born in Bristol, UK.
1836	Elizabeth Garrett is born in London, UK.
1842	The first surgical operation to use ether as an anaesthetic is performed.
1849	Elizabeth Blackwell graduates from Geneva Medical College.
1854	Florence Nightingale travels to the Crimea to nurse wounded soldiers.
1855	Mary Seacole sets up the "British Hotel" in the Crimea.
1865	Elizabeth Garrett is licensed to practise as a doctor.
1868	Elizabeth Blackwell founds a medical college for women.
1870	Louis Pasteur and Robert Koch prove that many diseases are caused by microscopic organisms.
1874	Elizabeth Garrett Anderson, Elizabeth Blackwell and others found the London School of Medicine for Women.
1881	Mary Seacole dies.
1882	Melanie Reizes (later Melanie Klein) is born in Vienna, Austria.
1895	X-rays are first used for medical imaging.

1901	Karl Landsteiner discovers the different human blood types.
1909	Rita Levi-Montalcini is born in Turin, Italy.
1909	Virginia Apgar is born in Westfield, New Jersey, USA.
1910	Elizabeth Blackwell dies.
1910	Florence Nightingale dies.
1917	Elizabeth Garrett Anderson dies.
1928	Alexander Fleming discovers the antibiotic penicillin.
1952	Virginia Apgar presents the first findings on the use of the Apgar score in childbirth.
1954	The first human kidney transplant is performed.
1960	Melanie Klein dies.
1974	Virginia Apgar dies.
1986	Rita Levi-Montalcini is awarded the Nobel Prize for her discovery of nerve growth factor.
2000	The Human Genome Project maps all human genes.
2012	Rita Levi-Montalcini dies.

Gallery

The scientists covered in this book are only a few of the women who have advanced the study of medicine, but here are more who achieved great things.

Florence Sabin (1871-1953)

An American scientist who did research on the brain, blood vessels and the lymphatic system. Florence became the first woman appointed as a full professor at Johns Hopkins University. In 1925 she became the first woman to be elected to the National Academy of Sciences.

Susan La Flesche Picotte (1865-1915)

A member of the Omaha tribe who became the first Native American to qualify as a medical doctor. Susan campaigned for land rights for Native Americans, as well as working to improve public health.

Maria Montessori (1870-1952)

An Italian teacher who developed a new system of education. She trained as a doctor before opening a preschool based on her educational ideas. She believed in independence and freedom (within limits) for children, and in allowing them to develop naturally.

Rebecca Lee Crumpler (1831-1895)

The first African American woman to become a doctor in the United States. As a doctor, she treated poor women and children in Boston and in Virginia. Rebecca later wrote a book about medical care for women and children.

Cicely Saunders (1918-2005)

Cicely Saunders trained as a nurse during World War II and later became a doctor and then a social worker. She set up the modern hospice movement, which looks after people who are dying. She was made a Dame of the British Empire in 1980.

Gerty Cori (1896-1957)

A Czech-born biochemist who emigrated to the United States. Working closely with her husband, Carl, she made important breakthroughs in understanding how the body breaks down sugars. Gerty and Carl won a Nobel Prize in 1947.

Rosalyn Sussman Yalow (1921-2011)

An American physicist who won a Nobel Prize in 1977 for developing a technique that allows scientists to measure tiny quantities of substances. It can be used on viruses and medicines in the body, allowing blood to be accurately screened.

SCIENCE NOW

Scientists are learning more about the body and how to treat disease. Many researchers are looking into how we can manipulate genes to make the body heal itself. Research into new medicines and surgical techniques is saving lives around the world.

There is still a lot to do. There are still no cures for many deadly diseases. In addition to medical researchers, we also need doctors on the ground who can treat patients. Could you have a career in medicine and health?

There are many resources available to help you learn about the human body. To keep up to date with all the latest medical discoveries, visit mrc.ukri.org. And to find out how to get into science, visit STEM information sites, such as the WISE campaign at **www.wisecampaign.org.uk**

Glossary

amputation cutting off a limb for medical reasons

anaesthesiology branch of science dealing with anaesthetics

anaesthetic drug that causes a loss of sensation, so that a patient cannot feel pain

antibiotic medicine that kills harmful microorganisms such as bacteria

apothecary person who prepares and sells medicines

depression mental disorder marked by severe sadness

dictatorship form of government in which one person has complete power

embryo an animal in the earliest stages of development, before birth

fascist following an extreme right-wing form of government

genetics branch of biology dealing with how traits are passed down

hygiene cleanliness and other practices that promote good health

nerve cell a type of cell that sends and receives messages

nervous system the system in the body that responds to stimuli. The brain, spinal cord and nerves make up this system

Nobel Prize prestigious prize awarded each year for achievements in different areas, including medicine

psychoanalysis a way of treating mental problems by exploring unconscious mental processes

pus yellowish fluid that leaks from a wound and contains bacteria

slavery system in which some people own others and force them to work without pay

statistics the collection and analysis of numerical data

surgeon doctor who specializes in performing operations

theory an idea that has not yet been proved

tumour a cancerous growth

unconscious not marked by conscious thought

Further resources

Books

Florence Nightingale (DK Life Stories), Kitson Jazynka (Dorling Kindersley, 2019)

Trailblazers: 33 Women in Science Who Changed the World, Rachel Swaby (Random House Books for Young Readers, 2016)

Women in Science: 50 Fearless Pioneers Who Changed the World, Rachel Ignotofsky (Wren & Rook, 2017)

The World's First Women Doctors: Elizabeth Blackwell and Elizabeth Garrett Anderson, Isabel Thomas (HarperCollins, 2015)

Websites

www.bbc.co.uk/history/historic_figures/garrett_anderson_elizabeth.shtml
Go here to learn more about Elizabeth Garrett Anderson.

www.healthguidance.org/entry/6355/1/Medical-History--Women-in-Medicine.html
This has a detailed history of female doctors.

www.sciencemuseum.org.uk/broughttolife/themes/practisingmedicine/women
This site provides information about the history of women in medicine.

time.com/4460720/virginia-apgar/
Find out more about Virginia Apgar and her work saving babies.

index